'09

Cc

MW01046385

Contents

written by John Lockyer

1

Caves are found high up in the mountains, under the sea, and deep under the earth. Some caves are only big enough for one person.

underwater cave

Other caves have long, twisting tunnels, and huge hollows. Rocks, lakes, waterfalls, streams, and tiny plants and animals are found inside caves.

Some caves are made by volcanoes. When lava flows out of a volcano, the surface cools down and turns into rock.

lava cave

The rock makes a tube around the hot lava inside. When the lava stops flowing, a big tunnel called a lava cave is left behind.

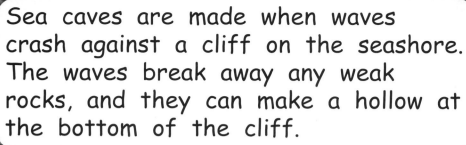

Sea caves are made when waves crash against a cliff on the seashore. The waves break away any weak rocks, and they can make a hollow at the bottom of the cliff.

sea cave

As more rocks are broken away, the hollow becomes a cave. Crabs, starfish, octopuses, seals, and sea lions make their homes in sea caves.

Ice caves are made by water that has frozen. In summer, some of the ice melts, and the cave opens up.

ice cave

In winter, the water freezes again, and the cave closes up. It is very, very cold inside an ice cave.

Most caves are found in limestone rock. Rainwater runs down through cracks in the rock, and it flows into underwater streams.

The rainwater slowly washes away the soft rock in any cracks, and it cuts out tunnels and caves. It takes thousands of years to make a limestone cave.

Many limestone caves have rock icicles. They are made by water dripping through cracks in the cave roof. Icicles that grow down from the cave roof are called stalactites.

icicles

Icicles that grow up from the cave floor are called stalagmites. Sometimes a stalagmite and a stalactite join and make a pillar.

Most caves are cold, damp, and dark. Some plants, like fungi, grow in caves because they don't need sunlight.

spider

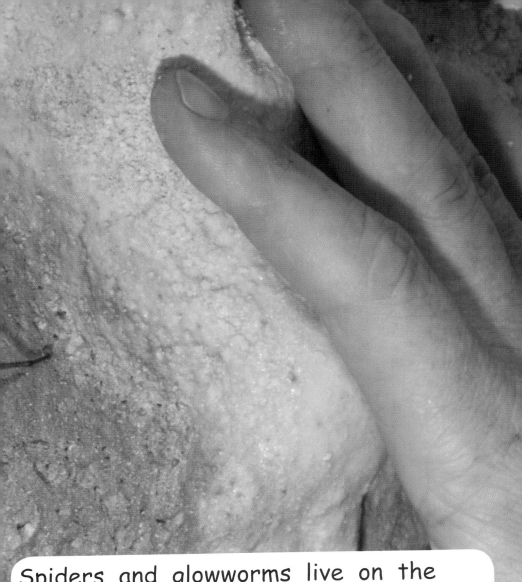

Spiders and glowworms live on the walls and roofs of some caves. Bats and bears use caves for sleeping and staying warm in the winter.

cave village

Many years ago, people lived in caves. They painted pictures on the walls and roofs. Caves were homes then, but now they are used for exploring.